HOW ARE THEY DIFFERENT?

Tell Me the DIFFERENCE Between a
RABBIT and a HARE

Leigh Rockwood

PowerKiDS press.

New York

Published in 2013 by The Rosen Publishing Group, Inc.
29 East 21st Street, New York, NY 10010

First Edition

Editor: Joanne Randolph
Book Design: Kate Laczynski

Photo Credits: Cover (rabbit), p. 9 (top) Cordier Sylvain/hemis.fr/Getty Images; cover (hare) nialat/Shutterstock.com; p. 4 Michael Connell/Flickr/Getty Images; pp. 5, 13 Peter Betts/Shutterstock.com; pp. 6, 10, 11, 21 iStockphoto/Thinkstock; p. 7 Martha Marks/Shutterstock.com; p. 9 (bottom) Erhard Nerger/Getty Images; p. 12 Alan Scheer/Shutterstock.com; p. 14 Four Oaks/Shutterstock.com; p. 15 Herbert Kratky/Shutterstock.com; p. 16 Craig K. Lorenz/Photo Researchers/Getty Images; p. 17 Laurent Renault/Shutterstock.com; p. 18 Patryk Kosmider/Shutterstock.com; p. 19 Konrad Wothe/Getty Images; p. 20 Mayovskyy Andrew/Shutterstock.com; p. 22 Joy Brown/Shutterstock.com.

Library of Congress Cataloging-in-Publication Data

Rockwood, Leigh.
 Tell me the difference between a rabbit and a hare / by Leigh Rockwood. — 1st ed.
     p. cm. — (How are they different?)
Includes index.
ISBN 978-1-4488-9638-7 (library binding) — ISBN 978-1-4488-9734-6 (pbk.) —
ISBN 978-1-4488-9735-3 (6-pack)
1. Rabbits—Juvenile literature. 2. Hares—Juvenile literature. I. Title.
QL737.L32R64 2013
599.32—dc23
                                        2012022308

Manufactured in the United States of America
CPSIA Compliance Information: Batch #W13PK5: For Further Information contact Rosen Publishing, New York, New York at 1-800-237-9932

CONTENTS

LET'S LOOK AT RABBITS AND HARES

At first glance, rabbits and hares are hard to tell apart. They are both **mammals** that are known for their soft fur and long ears. In fact, rabbits and hares belong to the same scientific family. It is called Leporidae. This

Rabbits live in many places around the world, but more than half the world population of rabbits lives in North America.

Notice the front legs and ears on this hare. Do you see that they are longer than those on the rabbit on the facing page?

family contains 54 **species** and includes rabbits, jackrabbits, and hares.

Rabbits and hares are closely related, but there are differences that make them easy to tell apart if you know what to look for. This book will teach you how to tell these two animals apart.

WHEN A RABBIT IS NOT A RABBIT

When looking at members of the Leporidae family, you are really looking at just two kinds of animals, rabbits and hares. That is because, in spite of the name, jackrabbits are actually hares. There are 32 species of what scientists call true hares, from the antelope jackrabbits of the southwestern

The black-tailed jackrabbit is actually a hare. Scientists believe that its extra large ears work to help the rabbit keep its body from becoming too hot or cold.

Cottontail rabbits are one of the most widespread rabbit species in North America and South America. They are known for the white, fluffy tails that give them their name.

United States to the arctic hares that live north of the Arctic Circle.

The other 22 species in this family are rabbits, from the tiny pygmy rabbit to the cottontail rabbits found across the United States. Some rabbits have the word "hare" in their names. That means you cannot tell rabbits and hares apart just by their names!

HOW ARE RABBITS AND HARES ALIKE?

Because they are part of the same scientific family, rabbits and hares have many things in common. They are both **herbivores**, or plant eaters, and have similar diets. They are **prey** animals, or animals that other animals like to eat for food. They have long ears and short tails. Both have eyes set on the sides of their heads to make it easier to keep a lookout for approaching **predators**, which they can then move quickly to avoid.

Rabbits and hares also have fur that they shed when the seasons change. In winter, the fur is thick. They shed this winter coat when the weather warms. The winter and summer coats of some rabbits and hares can even be a different color!

It is easy to see how, at first glance, it would be hard to tell apart a rabbit, such as the one above, and a hare, like this one on the right.

GET A LEG UP!

One of the first things you can do to tell the difference between a rabbit and a hare is to look at the legs. Both animals are strong jumpers and often travel in a zigzag pattern to escape from predators. Hares have longer legs and bigger feet than do rabbits, though.

A jackrabbit can not only run faster than many predators, it can also make leaps as long as 10 feet (3 m). This lets it easily clear any objects between itself and safety.

Rabbits have five claws on their front paws and four claws on their back paws. Rabbits use their legs to run, hop, and sometimes to dig. They also use them to thump the ground to warn other rabbits of danger.

This difference in leg length means a difference in how fast the two animals can move. A rabbit, such as the cottontail, can reach speeds of up to 18 miles per hour (29 km/h). A hare, such as the jackrabbit, can move as fast as 40 miles per hour (64 km/h)!

COMPARING RABBITS

SCIENTIFIC FAMILY	Leporidae
NUMBER OF SPECIES	22
LEGS	Shorter
EARS	Shorter
DIET	Herbivore
TOP SPEED	18 mph (29 km/h)
HOME	Burrow or warren
BABY NAME	Kitten
BABY FEATURES AT BIRTH	No fur, eyes closed, helpless for days

and HARES

Leporidae	**SCIENTIFIC FAMILY**
32	**NUMBER OF SPECIES**
Longer	**LEGS**
Longer, often with black markings	**EARS**
Herbivore	**DIET**
40 mph (64 km/h)	**TOP SPEED**
Form or nest	**HOME**
Leveret	**BABY NAME**
Fully furred, eyes open, can run within hours	**BABY FEATURES AT BIRTH**

Another way to tell the difference between a rabbit and a hare is to look at the animal's ears. Both animals have large ears and a very sharp sense of hearing, which helps warn them if a predator is approaching. Hares generally have longer ears than do rabbits, though. In addition, hares' ears have black fur on the tips.

This scrub hare lives in hot, dry places in southern Africa. Its ears are longer than hares that live in cooler climates.

14

Rabbits and hares can move their ears to gather sound. This helps them hear predators from any direction before it is too late.

Take a look at the ears of rabbits and hares from different **climates**. You will notice that species that live in warm climates generally have longer ears than ones that live in cold climates. The longer rabbits' and hares' ears are, the more heat they can let out of their bodies. This helps rabbits in warm climates stay cool and helps rabbits in cold climates stay warm.

15

LET'S EAT!

Although rabbits and hares are both herbivores, they do not have exactly the same diets. Their diets change throughout the year, too, depending on which plants are growing.

Rabbits prefer to eat softer plant matter, such as grasses, leaves, ferns, stems, and vegetables.

This jackrabbit stands on its hind legs to nibble on some twigs.

Rabbits can often be seen in meadows or backyards in the early evenings or mornings eating clover and other plants.

This is why many gardeners see rabbits as pests. Hares eat leaves and plant shoots. They also eat a greater amount of tougher foods than rabbits, such as buds from flowering plants, tree bark, and twigs.

RABBIT AND HARE HABITATS

Many kinds of rabbits live in burrows or warrens. The burrow gives them a safe place to rest when they are not looking for food.

Rabbits and hares live in a wide range of **habitats** and are found on every continent except Antarctica. There are species of rabbits and hares living in forests, grasslands, deserts, mountains, and swamps. Rabbits tend to live in places where there are more bushes, trees, and places to take cover, while hares are more often found in open places with less cover.

Although they are found in many of the same habitats, rabbits and hares make different homes for themselves there. Rabbits are more likely to live in groups and to dig burrows or warrens in which to live. Hares are more likely to live alone and build forms, or flattened hare-shaped depressions in the ground.

This arctic hare rests in its form. Arctic hares live in cold habitats. They have shorter ears and thick fur to keep them warm. Their fur turns white in winter to help them blend in with snowy surroundings.

Rabbits and hares may **mate** several times each year. This depends on how much food is available. For this reason, rabbits and hares living in harsh climates like the Arctic may mate only once a year.

Baby hares rest in their form for much of the day. Their mothers visit them only once a day for about 5 minutes to feed them.

Some kinds of rabbits make underground nests for their babies. These nests can be part of a group den, or the mother may dig a separate breeding tube in which to raise her babies.

Rabbit and hare litters generally have between three and eight babies. Baby rabbits are called kittens, while baby hares are called leverets. Leverets are born with fur, open eyes, and can run just a few hours after being born. Kittens are born hairless, with closed eyes, and can move around when they are a few days old. Rabbit and hare mothers **nurse** their young for a few weeks. Within a couple of months, the young of most rabbit and hare species can take care of themselves.

NOW YOU KNOW!

One place you will see only rabbits and never hares is at a pet store. There are rabbits that have been **domesticated** as pets, but there is no such thing as a pet hare!

Many people keep domesticated rabbits as pets. Like any pet, rabbits need the proper care to do well.

Now you know about the different characteristics that scientists look at to group rabbits and hares. The next time you catch a glimpse of a long-eared animal in your backyard, you will know if it is a rabbit or a hare.

GLOSSARY

climates (KLY-muts) The kind of weather certain places have.

domesticated (duh-MES-tih-kayt-ed) Raised to live with people.

habitats (HA-buh-tats) The surroundings where animals or plants naturally live.

herbivores (ER-buh-vorz) Animals that eat only plants.

mammals (MA-mulz) Warm-blooded animals that have backbones and hair, breathe air, and feed milk to their young.

mate (MAYT) To come together to make babies.

nurse (NURS) When a female feeds her baby milk from her body.

predators (PREH-duh-terz) Animals that kill other animals for food.

prey (PRAY) An animal that is hunted by another animal for food.

species (SPEE-sheez) One kind of living thing. All people are one species.

INDEX

WEBSITES

Due to the changing nature of Internet links, PowerKids Press has developed an online list of websites related to the subject of this book. This site is updated regularly. Please use this link to access the list: www.powerkidslinks.com/hatd/raha/